Stories of Jesus

Written by Leena Lane   Illustrated by Roma Bishop

The First Christmas

Clip-clop, went the donkey's hooves on the stony road. The donkey was tired. Mary and Joseph were tired. They had traveled all the way from Nazareth to Bethlehem to be counted by the Romans.

Mary was soon going to have a baby. But when they reached Bethlehem, there was nowhere to stay. Every innkeeper turned them away, saying, "Sorry! We're full up!"

Finally, Joseph knocked on the door of one last inn. There was no room here either, but the innkeeper showed them to a place where the animals slept. Mary had her baby, wrapped him in strips of cloth and put him in a manger.

An angel had told Mary that her baby would be very special – God's own son – and she should call him Jesus.

On the hills near Bethlehem, shepherds were watching over their sheep. God sent an angel to give them an important message.

"Do not be afraid. Jesus, God's own son, has been born in Bethlehem. Go and find the baby Jesus. He is lying in a manger."

The sky was bright with dazzling light and a whole host of angels sang:

"Glory to God in the highest!"
The shepherds were amazed. They hurried down to the town.

When the shepherds reached the town, they found Jesus lying in a manger, just as the angel had said. They went back to their sheep, singing praises to God.

A LITTLE PRAYER

Thank you, Lord, for sending Jesus to be born on earth. Thank you that we can know him too.

The Baby King

One night long ago, some wise men saw a bright new star in the sky.

"This star means that somewhere on earth a *baby king* has been born," they said to each other. "We must visit him."

They set out, following the star.
At last they came to Jerusalem,
where King Herod lived.
"Where is the *baby king*?" they asked.
King Herod called together his own wise men.
"What do you know about a *baby king*?" he asked.
"Years ago, God promised that a special child would be born in Bethlehem," they replied.

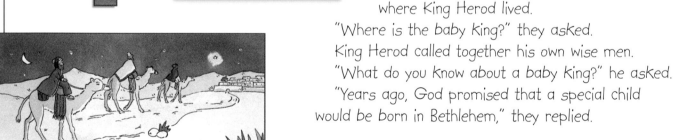

The wise men set out again
on their weary camels.
In the town of Bethlehem,
right above a house,
the star stood still in the sky.

The wise men went into the house.
They found the baby Jesus with his mother,
Mary. They knelt down to worship him.
At last they had found the baby King.
They gave him their presents – shining gold,
sweet frankincense, and costly myrrh.

They set off for home joyfully.
They were glad they had made
the long journey, because they
had seen Jesus, the baby King.

A LITTLE PRAYER

Thank you, Lord, that the wise men worshiped you.
Help us to love and worship you too.

Jesus and his Friends

One day Jesus was standing on the shore of the lake. Crowds of people had come to listen to him telling them about God.

Jesus saw two fishing boats pulled up on the beach. The fishermen were washing their nets.

Jesus got into a boat belonging to Simon Peter and asked him to push the boat out a short way. Jesus spoke to the crowds from the boat.

When Jesus had finished speaking, he said to Simon, "Push the boat out to the deeper water and catch some fish."

"But we fished all night and caught nothing!" said Simon.

"Let down the nets," said Jesus.

So the fishermen let down the nets. They caught so many fish that the nets nearly *broke*! James and John came over from the other *boat* and helped them. The boats nearly sank with the weight of the fish!

The fishermen – Simon Peter, Andrew, James, and John – were amazed!

"Now come with me," said Jesus. "I will make you fishers of men."

The fishermen left their nets and followed Jesus.

These were the first of Jesus' special friends, called disciples.

A LITTLE PRAYER

Thank you, God, for choosing ordinary people to be your special friends.
Thank you that I can be your friend.

A Hole in the Roof

There was a man near
Capernaum who couldn't walk.
He lay on his mat every day.
One day, four friends came to see him.
"Jesus has come to our town!" they said.
"I wish I could see him," said the man on his mat.
He knew Jesus could make people better. Could he help him to walk again?

"We'll take you to Jesus," said the man's friends.
They carried him on his mat to where Jesus was.
    But there was a huge crowd of people outside the house.
    "We'll never get through this crowd," they said.
    Then one of them had a good idea.

The friends carried the man up the steps outside the house and on to the roof.
    Then they began to dig through the mud and branches.
    Soon there was a big hole.
    The friends carefully lowered the man down on his mat.
    The people below were very surprised!

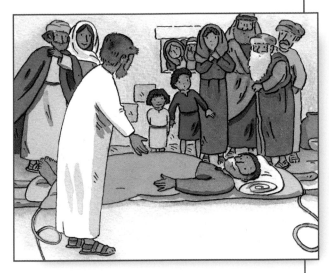

Jesus looked up at the four men
peering down through the hole in the roof.
Jesus looked at the man on his mat.
　　Then Jesus said to the man, "Get up.
Pick up your mat and go home."

The man tried to move.
　　For the first time, he was able to move his
feet, then his legs. Then he could stand up!
　　The man rolled up his mat and walked out of
the house.
　　He was so happy he said thank you to God.
And the four friends were very happy that they
had helped the man to meet Jesus.

A LITTLE PRAYER

Dear God, thank you for helping the man
to walk. Thank you that you can do
incredible things!

The Dreadful Storm

One day Jesus and his friends got into a boat on the lake. Jesus was tired. It had been a busy day.

"Let's go over to the other side of the lake," said Jesus.

 Suddenly a fierce storm blew up and the boat was tossed about like a cork. The waves began to splash into the boat. Jesus' friends were terrified of sinking.

But Jesus was fast asleep in the boat.

"Save us, Lord!" they shouted to Jesus. "We're going to drown!"

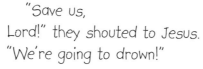

Jesus sat up.

"Why are you so afraid?" he said.

Then Jesus got up and ordered the wind and the waves to calm down.
The storm vanished.

Everyone was amazed!
"Even the winds and the waves obey him!" said his friends. Jesus had saved them all from the storm.

A LITTLE PRAYER

Thank you, Jesus, that you care about big things and little things.
Help me to tell you when I am frightened.

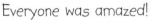

The Little Girl who was Ill

Jairus only had one daughter. She was twelve years old. She had become very ill and Jairus didn't know what to do.

He heard that Jesus was in the town and could make people well again. Jairus hurried to find Jesus in the crowds.
"Please help me!" he begged. "My little girl is very ill. She might die."

Jesus was very busy, helping an old lady in the crowd. She had been ill for twelve years and no doctors could help her. Now Jesus had made her well again!

Suddenly a messenger came from Jairus' house.

"It's too late. Your daughter has died!" he said. Jairus was very upset. But Jesus told him not to worry.

"Just believe, and she will be well," he said to Jairus.

He went to Jairus' house and saw the little girl lying on a bed.

"She is not dead," said Jesus. "She is only sleeping."

"Get up, my child!" he said. And suddenly the little girl sat up! She was alive and well again.

"Give her something to eat," said Jesus. Her parents could not believe their eyes! Their little girl was alive again!

A LITTLE PRAYER

Thank you, Jesus, for making the little girl better. Thank you that you can do amazing things.

The Big Picnic

Jesus was once speaking to a large crowd of people. They had been listening to him all day and were getting hungry.

"Where can we find enough to feed all these people?" Jesus asked Philip.

"It would cost more than two hundred silver coins," said Philip.

Andrew came up to Jesus.
   "There's a young boy here with a packed lunch," he said. "He has five barley loaves and two fish. But that's not enough to feed everyone."

Jesus told all the people to sit down on the grass. He took the five loaves and two fishes from the boy.

Jesus then did something wonderful! He shared the food with all the people.

No one went away hungry. Jesus gave them all enough to eat, and there were even twelve baskets full of left-overs.

Jesus had fed more than five thousand people with just five loaves and two fishes. What a fantastic picnic!

A LITTLE PRAYER

Thank you, Jesus, for feeding all the people with a boy's packed lunch. Thank you, Jesus, that you can use even the small things we give you and make them special.

The Lost Sheep

One day, Jesus came to a town and told a story to the crowd of people gathered round him:

"There was once a man who had a hundred sheep. He knew them all by name and took good care of them. At night he counted them as they went in through the gate to make sure they were all there. But one night, there were only ninety-nine.

One sheep was missing.

"The sheep had wandered away and now it was lost. 'I must find it,' the shepherd said.

So he left the other sheep in the fold and went out into the night.

"The shepherd walked and walked, listening for the cry of a lost sheep. When he found it, it was so tired it could hardly stand up. So the shepherd picked it up and carried it home.

The shepherd was so happy that he invited all his friends to a party.

'Come and celebrate!' he said. 'I've found my lost sheep!'"

When Jesus had finished the story, he said, "Sometimes people do bad things and lose their way. But God still loves them. God wants to find them again, and when they are found, God is as happy as the shepherd who found his lost sheep."

A LITTLE PRAYER

Thank you, God, that to you I am as special as the shepherd's lost sheep. Thank you for loving me so much.

The Lost Son

Jesus once told this story to show
how much God loves us:

"There was a man who had two sons. The younger
son grew bored of living with his family. He had
heard that there were exciting places in other
countries. He wanted to go exploring. So he asked
his dad for his share of his riches, and set off.

"His father was very sad that his son had
gone away. He loved his son very much and
hoped he would return.

"Meanwhile, the son spent all the money very quickly.
There was a shortage of food in the land and he had
no money left for food. Nobody wanted to be his friend
any more. He had to find a job, feeding pigs.

"There was no food for him to eat. He was so hungry he nearly ate the pigs' food!

'I must go home,' he thought. 'Perhaps Dad will let me work on his farm.'

"As he came near to his old home, he saw his dad running towards him. He was shouting, 'Welcome home!' and gave him a great big hug.

"The father gave a special party for his son, with music and dancing. He thought he had lost him, but the son he loved had come back. How happy that made him!"

A LITTLE PRAYER

Thank you, God, for loving us like the father in the story.

Jesus and the Children

Some people wanted to take their little children and babies to see Jesus. They wanted him to bless them by placing his hands on their heads.

But some of Jesus' friends tried to stop people bringing their children to Jesus.

"Don't bother him," they said.

When Jesus heard them saying this, he became angry. Jesus thought children were very special.

"Let the children come and see me and don't try to stop them," he said.

"The Kingdom of heaven belongs to those who love me like these children do," said Jesus.

Jesus took the children and babies in his arms, placed his hands on them and said a special blessing. He wanted them to know how much he loved them all.

A LITTLE PRAYER

Thank you, Jesus, that everyone matters to you. No one is too small.
    Thank you for loving me.

The Man in the Tree

There was once a man called Zacchaeus. He was a tax collector. But when he collected the money, he made people pay too much. Nobody liked him.

One day, Zacchaeus saw crowds in the street.

"Jesus is coming to our town!" they shouted.

Zacchaeus had heard about Jesus. More than anything else, Zacchaeus wanted to meet him.

Zacchaeus was not very tall, and the street was crowded. No one would let him through.

Then he had an idea. There was a big tree not far away. He decided to climb it. When at last he reached a good strong branch, he peered down through the leaves.

He was just in time! Jesus was coming down the street. Jesus suddenly stopped and looked up.

"Come down here, Zacchaeus," he said. "I want to visit your house today."

Zacchaeus was so surprised, he almost fell out of the tree. Jesus knew his name. Jesus wanted to be his friend!

When Zacchaeus got down, he looked at Jesus. And all at once he remembered the bad things he had done. Suddenly he said, "I will give half my money to people who don't have enough. And I will pay back all the money I stole."

The crowd went silent. They stared in amazement.

Jesus smiled. "That's good," he said. "Now you are one of God's friends."

A LITTLE PRAYER

Thank you, Lord, for forgiving Zacchaeus.
Thank you that you forgive me when I say sorry too.

Jesus the King

One day Jesus told two of his friends, "Go to the village over there. You will find a young donkey that has never been ridden. Say that the Master needs it and bring it to me."

So the friends went to find the donkey. They untied it and brought it to Jesus and threw their cloaks over the donkey's back.

Jesus sat on the donkey's back and rode into Jerusalem.

Crowds of people threw their cloaks on the road where the donkey walked. They pulled palm branches off the trees and spread them in the road.

Everyone began to wave and shout and cheer for Jesus:
"Hurray! Praise God! Bless our King!"
Thinking Jesus was the king they had been waiting for, they all welcomed him into Jerusalem.

A LITTLE PRAYER

Dear Jesus, help me to praise you too.

Jesus is Alive!

Jesus' friends were very upset. Jesus had healed the sick, given the blind their sight, fed the hungry, blessed the children. But Jesus had been put on the cross to die, and his body had been placed in a tomb.

Early on Sunday morning, some of the women went to take special spices to the tomb. They had a big shock! The large stone which blocked the entrance to the tomb had been rolled away!

Inside the tomb, Jesus' body had gone. All that was left were strips of cloth which the body had been wrapped in. Suddenly two men in bright shining clothes appeared.

"Don't be afraid!" they said. "I know you are looking for Jesus, but he is not here any more. He is alive!"

The women couldn't believe it! They ran home at once and told all Jesus' friends.

"Jesus is alive! Jesus is alive!"

Very soon they saw Jesus again for themselves. It was true! Jesus was alive!

A LITTLE PRAYER

Thank you, God, that Jesus came alive again! Thank you that he is still alive today!

Published in the United States of America by
Abingdon Press, 201 Eighth Avenue South, Nashville, Tennessee 37203

ISBN 0-687-06537-2

First edition 2003

Copyright © 2003 AD Publishing Services Ltd
1 Churchgates, The Wilderness, Berkhamsted, Herts HP4 2UB
Text copyright © 2003 AD Publishing Services Ltd, Leena Lane
Illustrations copyright © 2003 Roma Bishop

References for Bible stories
The First Christmas: Luke 2:1-20
The Baby King: Matthew 2:1-11
Jesus and his Friends: Luke 5:1-11
A Hole in the Roof: Luke 5:17-26
The Dreadful Storm: Luke 8:22-25
The Little Girl who was Ill: Luke 8:40-56
The Big Picnic: John 6:1-15
The Lost Sheep: Luke 15:1-7
The Lost Son: Luke 15:11-32
Jesus and the Children: Mark 10:13-16
The Man in the Tree: Luke 19:1-10
Jesus the King: Luke 19:28-38
Jesus is Alive!: Luke 24:1-12

Printed and bound in Singapore